Family Plowing

AND OTHER PRAIRIE POEMS:
NEW AND USED

A MEADOWLARK BOOK

Meadowlark (an imprint of Chasing Tigers Press)
meadowlark-books.com
P.O. Box 333, Emporia, KS 66801

Cover Image by Duane L. Herrmann

ISBN: 978-1-7322410-9-1

Library of Congress Control Number: 2019950068

*"The country is the world of the soul,
the city is the world of bodies"*

-Bahá'u'lláh

Also by Duane L. Herrmann

Ninety Years in Kansas, Buffalo Press, 1987[+]

Early Poems: a Retrospective with Notes, Buffalo Press, 1989[+*]

Whispers Shouting Glory, Buffalo Press, 1989[+*]

Fasting: A Bahá'í Handbook (comp.), George Ronald, publisher, 1989

Voices From a Borrowed Garden (ed.), Buffalo Press, 1989[*]

Robert Hayden Poetry Fellowship, Louhelen Center, 1989

Andrew Herrmann Family in America, Buffalo Press, 1990[+]

Die Familia Andrew Herrmann in Amerika, Reckendorf, Deutschland, 1994[+]

Statements on Writing (comp.), Buffalo Press, 1993[+]

The Bahá'í Faith in Kansas, since 1897, Buffalo Press, 1994[+]

The Life of May Brown, in her own words, Buffalo Press, 1994[+]

Fragrances of Grace, Buffalo Press, 1996[+*]

Early Bahá'ís of Enterprise, Buffalo Press, 1997[+]

A History of the Bahá'í Community of Samarkand, Buffalo Press, 1999[+]

Ninety-five Years in Topeka, Buffalo Press, 2001[+]

'Abdu'l-Bahá Writes to Kansas City, no publisher, 2002[+]

A Little History of Islam in Topeka, no publisher, 2003[+]

Prairies of Possibilities, iUniverse, 2005.[*]

By Thy Strengthening Grace, Buffalo Press, 2006
—Ferguson Kansas History Book Award, 2007—

Sweet Scented Streams, no publisher, 2011[+*]

Hidden Meanings in the Poetry of Robert Hayden, Buffalo Press, 2012+

Blessings of Teaching, Mirat Publications, 2014

Ichnographical: 173, Delamater–Moore–Curtis, 2016[*]

In Praise of Prairies, Origami Poems, 2017[++*]

Praise the King of Glory, Buffalo Press, 2017[*]

Escape from Earth: the journal of a planetary pioneer, Czykmate, ebook: 2018, print: 2019

Gedichte aus Prairies of Possibilities: Deutsch und Englisch, Buffalo Press, 2019

* poetry   + chapbook   ++microchapbook

Family Plowing

AND OTHER PRAIRIE POEMS:
NEW AND USED

Duane L. Herrmann

CONTENTS

Family Plowing 1
Grandfather's Road 2
Spring Lake 3
Chicken Creek Road 4
Spring Towers 5
Night Necklaces 6
Pigs in a Blanket... 7
House on the Edge of a Meadow 8
The Wind's Own 9
The Family House 11
Magic Evening 12
Lost Road 13
Tiny Pond 14
Plowing Lesson 15
Coyote Rules the World 16
Kansas Nachtlied, Goethe 17
Summer Wetting 18
Prairie Hawk.. 19
Witness.. 20
Making Hay.. 21
Grandfather's Barn.. 22
For Deer Waiting... 23
Song of the Prairie Night.................................... 24
Wagon Tale 25
On the Horizon 26
Builders of Barns.. 27
Unnatural Mark 28
Sleeping to the Sound of Rain.............................. 29
Barn Remains 30
Next Five Exits... 31
Buffalo Surprise 32
Absence by Inference... 33
Garden Effort 34
On the Hillside 35

Road Through the Trees 36
Stone Shell 37
The Fullness of Summer 38
Tree Dance 39
Rolling Seas 40
Dawn Light 41
Traveling 42
Caught in the Air 43
Flint Hills Farm 44
Spirit of the Well 45
Haunting Summons 46
Cottonwood 47
Moving Water 48
Buffalo Spirit 49
Country Buried 51
Night Secrets 52
Rural Conversation 53
Transition 54
Pasture Gate 55
Schoolhouse Picnic 56
Sky Vast 57
Pond Experiment 58
Wind Blown 59
Ancient Water 60
Rain Dance 61
Testing the Tree 62
Fence Building 63
Challenge of the Bridge 64
The Sky 65
Time Has Told 66
Prairie Breath 67
Golden 68
Evening Meditation 69
Silo Sentinel 70
Autumn Messengers 71
Traces that Remain 72
Night Coming 73
Decision to Honor 74
October Forever! 75

No Mountain Lions 76
Autumn Wind Speaks 77
Lonely Land 78
Seeds 79
Autumn Afternoon 80
Remaining Witness 81
Clearing Cedars 82
Winter Wet 83
My Father's Eyes 84
Bluebird Winter 85
Snow Falling 86
Snow Makes Clear 87
Winter Rodent Dreams 88
Fire in the Snow 89
Snow Reveals 90
In the Snow 91
Fire in Snowlight 92
Warning 93
The Flower Dreams 94
Too Cold 95
Waiting for Spring 96
Haunting Hope of Spring 97

Notes 99
Index of Titles 101
Index of First Lines 103
Publication Credits 105
About the Author 107

FAMILY PLOWING

I plow the paper with a pen
engaged as the family has been
in cultivation: sowing and reaping.

I plow the paper with a pen,
in a solitary field—
it always has been.

My father was a farmer,
his father, and his before him;
we are plowmen in our rows.

I plow the paper with a pen—
rows of words across the space
in neat and even lines.

Though plowing is the family business,
my "machineries" now differ
for a different kind of crop.

But the plowing is the same:
long straight lines
across unmarked fields.

GRANDFATHER'S ROAD

Invisible to the traveler now,
    two tracks through the grass,
but the discerning eye
    can see two fence rows on each side.

Across the prairie and down
    the hill it leads
over a little cement bridge,
    with iron rails;

One missing.
    Also missing is the house
and barn and windmill.
    Not even a line of stones.

His early life,
    his boyhood home,
has returned to the prairie
    from whence it came.

The earth
    reclaimed it's own.

But the road remains
    to show the way
to the past of my grandfather's life:
    he walked this way to school.

SPRING LAKE

Sitting on the rocks
    on the edge of the lake,
water gently claps
    into holes and spaces.

Breeze bringing waves
    brings ancient sounds
that have survived
    the post-columbian age:

Thumping, thumping, rhythmic thumping
    drums and chants:
in clear and ringing tones
    through the opposite trees.

The chants of America:
    native words in native voices,
five hundred years endured,
    proudly raised once more.

In clear evening sky
    the night queen sails,
smiles on children of the moon,
    knowing they will shine once more.

CHICKEN CREEK ROAD

No up-scale suburb, this!
"Chicken Creek Road"
named because of—what?

Obviously:
chickens in the creek.
At least
at some memorable moment.

Possibilities
are wild:
chickens everywhere!
up and down the creek!

This is:
local color,
a homespun name,
not to be easily forgotten.

Who could ever forget
an address on—
Chicken Creek Road?

SPRING TOWERS

Towers of the Spring,
   rising billowy brown
   climbing high in the sky...

Hundreds of feet in the air.
   One here, and another there,
   another further on...

Altering the landscape,
   dwarfing trees and hills,
   on the scale of clouds.

On the plains
   they can be seen for miles,
   awesome and unique.

Tomorrow they are gone,
   vanished in the air;
   blackened earth remains

Evidence
   of regeneration
   by prairie burning.

NIGHT NECKLACES

Glittering strings
strewn across hillsides.
Large and small
flaming jewels
form lines and loops
here and there,
up, down, around.
At night the sight
is awesome to behold.
Darkness hides
grass from ash
and contrasts
smoke towering high
lit by flames
illuminating,
reflecting,
necklaces
adorning hillsides
in prairie spring.

PIGS IN A BLANKET

Not a blanket, actually,
    but a towel, or several.
We wrapped the pigs in them
    to conserve their warmth.
They were tiny, born too early,
    and could easily die.
The mother, with her bulk,
    four—five hundred pounds,
could easily crush them
    and not even notice:
they were so tiny,
    she was so huge.
And the barn was cold, so cold,
    and freezing wind blew through,
they could not live there
    and would surely die,
so we wrapped them snug
    and put them on the open oven door.

HOUSE ON THE EDGE OF A MEADOW

There is a house,
  a tiny house,
sitting on the edge of a meadow.

A round silver egg:
  it is the scene of visions.

Tender young trees
  nestle it softly
so the breeze will not die.

Trips here,
  to read, write and pray,
  lead away to vast spaces.

My Heart Sings.

To have a tiny house
  is to be real
    for a tiny time,
in the woods
  on the edge of a meadow;

The sky is huge!

THE WIND'S OWN

Wind:
    roaring, howling—
      wild, screaming
    shrieking into every crack—
        shrilly, demonically.

Wind:
      incessantly calling—
        pleading, pulling, prying;
    never letting up—
      continually, mercilessly.

Alone—
    on the hill, the woman stood;
      surrounded by the wind
      crying though the grasses—
        pushing the clouds along.

She tried to see a house,
      or person,
    but no,
  she was alone,
    no other human evidence.

Alone—
    no one for miles—
      Just grass and hills and wind.
        her mate away to pay the claim
      she joined the wind.
shrieking, howling, crying…
      she was sister to the wind.
    They ran the hills together:
      companions.   >>>

The wind had claimed its own.

Up and down, she ran and rolled,
                    stumbled,
            unaware—
        and ran again.

Crying, shrieking…
            she was found
                    running with the wind.

No human here,
        she fought loving arms around her:

            a creature of the wind.

        She has her peace now,
    the wind does not trouble her
        on the Hill of Silence—
                caressed
            by the breeze.

THE FAMILY HOUSE

I sought refuge
    in the family house:
with walls of stone and love.

No screaming there
    but hugs
and twinkling eyes.

Windows rattle
    by blasts of wind,
but I was safe within.

Sheltered by trees
    open to breeze
with grass to play

I grew up
    but never away
from the house and farm.

Caring hands
    and listening eyes
Welcome me back home.

MAGIC EVENING

Grandmother engineered the evening
without her children knowing:
"Yes, bring the grandkids over."
(four)
"No, I'm not going anywhere."
(one)
"Would you like to leave the children?"
(four more)
"That will be fine."
She smiled.

She did not hint to any
that she would be watching
the other's children also.

One by one the cars stopped by
unloading children two by two.
When the last exclaimed,
"You should have told me..."
"Go on, have a good time,
we'll be fine."

And we *were* fine:

All the cousins in one room
paired by age or interest
(the oldest read a book);
There was nothing for Granma to do
but survey children wall to wall
and beam with joy
on that magic, blissful evening,
when life was as it should be—
one last moment of perfection,

not knowing that soon her son would die.

LOST ROAD

After the war of 1812,
not the European one,
the white man's hand
cut up the land
and gave this piece
to a widow of the war.
Natives who called this, "home,"
had been removed
never to return.
Several owners later
it was first farmed.
Decades more, a family stayed
and made the farm succeed,
then my parents bought it
and now a part is mine.
Despite my childhood here
surprises still await,
though I knew about the well
it was the road,
in the side of the hill,
that astonished me.
Nearly erased by erosion
trees now hide
what it once was
a century ago,
but—who made it,
and—where does it go?

TINY POND

No one would know
you were there
or had been;
cattails growing
in the damp
where water stands
and banks all grassy
with some weeds.
Birds fly over
and nest,
and frogs remain.
The only sign
of the one-time pond
is the dam
still stretching
from side to side
no longer able
to retain
its water.

PLOWING LESSON

I was fourteen
just learning to farm—
my first plowing lesson,
driving a tractor
only the summer before.
Father examined my effort:
"Plow to the edge of the field
then raise the plow to turn."
So I did
and swiped the only tree—
front axel bent:
tires angled to a V.
Thoughtful, my father looked
and swiped again the tree—
re-bending the axel
straight!
Then he left me
to finish plowing the field!

COYOTE RULES THE WORLD

As he trots across the field,
    along the fencerow,
    or down the dusty track;
Coyote is disdainful of the world:
    barking dogs,
    or passing car.
Gone are buffalo and open spaces
    but, no matter
    he will adapt.
He knows he is the only one
    who really matters…
    calling in the night.
His world secure and timeless,
    always mice and rabbits,
    and a wily brain.
Perennial prairie resident
    will take more than progress
    to force his kind away.

KANSAS NACHTLIED, GOETHE

There is a stillness
   over the hills and fields;
meadows lie baking
   in the heat.

There is no breath.

Birds are silent and the weeds
   grow lank and seed.

Wait!

The heat will feel you too.

SUMMER WETTING

Heat had been forever:
    constant oven-wind
    shriveled leaves and trees.

Cemented soil cracked
    in canyons reaching deep
    into the tortured earth.

No rain for more than weeks;
    moisture only dimly
    a faint and fragrant memory.

Suddenly from far away
    echoed muffled rumblings,
    and low dark clouds.

Salvation seemed too true
    to suspend parched lips
    or slack dry skin.

Eyes watched with hope and wonder
    as clouds relieved the sky
    from the searing sun.

A miraculous wall of wet
    advanced across the fields
    and, suddenly, was here!

God was good again.
    Steady showering filled
    pores and cracks and leaves.

The crops and life and animals
    were saved. The family
    would survive another year.

PRAIRIE HAWK

Over the fields and prairie
    creeks and tree lines
endless miles
    of countryside,
I survey my domain,
    All MINE! All MINE!
The wind past my eyes
    lifts me up or down.
A sound carries
    on the wind
and I know
    food is near.
I see motion
    and swoop down,
the meal...
    will be mine.

AH!
    Life is good!

WITNESS

Abandon building
    gray
weathered wood and warped
    still
erect, upright and proud
    here
on the side of the ridge,
    now
prairie all around - lonely,
    once
the seat of culture-learning
    pride
to become "Americans"
    this
was their school and center
    when
they knew who they were
    becoming.

MAKING HAY

Mornings when the dew had dried
  Granpa mowed the field of hay
  going round and round and round,
    outside to center.
Early after lunch the boy would rake
  the now dry hay
  once around for Granpa's twice,
    outside to center.
Fluffed up windrows snaked along
  from sheets of new cut grass
  raking opposite the cutting,
    outside to center.
Once done, the hay was raked again
  merging two windrows to one,
  drying all sides of the grass,
    outside to center.
Father ran the baler, especially—
  if the knotter had a temper,
  following the windrow
    outside to center

GRANDFATHER'S BARN

My grandfather's barn
    was huge, marvelously huge,
the largest building
    that I knew—
the entire upper floor
    was one HUGE room!
Much larger than my house,
    or even Granma's too!
Sunlight filtered in
    between the batten boards,
so it was always light
    and dust motes float.
The lower walls were rock
    with low beams.
Here the cows were milked
    and it was warm in winter.
One hundred years old
    the roof line sagged:
this—my grandfather's world,
    his kingdom and his keep.

FOR DEER WAITING

In twilight time
    cicada circus sings
        and fireflies alight.
A distant dog wakes
    and gentle jet rumbles
        through the clouds.
Darkness hides the day.
    I sit, watch and wait,
        for deer coming.
Slowly, from the woods,
    one step, then two,
        the doe ventures.
Sensing calm and safety,
    she walks
        into the field and nibbles.
Unexpectedly the fawn
    dances into sight
        and darkness hides away.

SONG OF THE PRAIRIE NIGHT

Howling, calling,
yipping joy:
coyotes all around
in communion.
Others too
join their songs:
owls in speech,
sleepy birds,
while more
rustle grass
as they pass.
Wind stirs trees—
bending branches
whispering secrets
of the leaves.
Insect chorus
whirrs and chirps
while deer
sleep soundly
hidden safe
in grass and brush.
Clouds slip silent
in and out
while the moon
smiles over all
and stars
move silent by.

WAGON TALE

Driving down the rocky road
   something soon "feels" different
then a crashing in the bushes.
   Backward glance saw horror:

Brand newbuilt hay wagon,
   shiny, clean and perfect,
just finished days ago;
   now awkward in the ditch.

Heart with dread the boy confessed
   the accident on reaching home.
The father, solemn, listens
   with simply nodding head.

He seems to take loss well,
   thought the son,
all thumbs when working
   farm tools and equipment.

At the scene they start to clear
   brush to free the wagon.
"This has grown up some," says the Dad,
   "since I last lost a wagon here."

ON THE HORIZON

Tree on the rise of the prairie
    stands tall,
etched against the sky
    it is seen for miles
a solitary witness
    to life before and after.
This tree sees raindrops
    and the wind
as companions
    with stars and grass.
Tree says:
    "I'm alive, I'm here, I'm now."
For "now"
    is the only time that is.
Now is the time we each have,
    the only time
to make our lives
    and save our souls.

BUILDERS OF BARNS

They knew,
   the builders of barns,
that the barn
   was the heart of the farm,
so they built them
   solid, to last:
stone foundations,
   sturdy wood above,
and painted red
   since it was cheap,
colorful and caught
   the landscape eye.
They built them strong
   to last a hundred years
for the farm to go on and on
   with the family forever,
never thinking that someday...
   the barns would die.

UNNATURAL MARK

Straight line
across the prairie
up and down
gently
to the horizon
miles and miles away
going somewhere in Kansas,
looks like nowhere,
trees here, there,
like shrubs,
distant, low,
where water runs
when it rains
and grass,
endless grass,
with wildflowers,
and above…
endless deep blue sky.

SLEEPING TO THE SOUND OF RAIN

On the vast dry plains
the sound of rain
is music to the soul,
more melodious
than angel's song
yet angels sing
of joy, renewal,
life and hope
with dropping rain.
Angels dance
and hearts sing
for rain is life
on the dusty land
and all rejoice
to hear the fall
of angel's rain
on dry plains.

BARN REMAINS

Trees have grown around it now
  in a pasture,
no house or drive—
  family gone
and children too,
  the wilderness reclaims...
The roof is gone,
  and upper walls and floor,
solid, rock foundation walls
  only remain
of a once magnificent
  barn.
The grand entrance,
  an awesome arch,
centered
  in one remaining wall.
Now only cows
  admire mason's skill.

NEXT FIVE EXITS

On the small state highway,
  Number Seventy-seven,
to be exact,
  and rural all the way,
the sign says,
  when entering a town:
"Matfield Green—
  Next Five Exits."

The town has five streets
  that cross the highway
so all are "exits"
  into the town,
just like any respectable
  megalopolis!

Who says country hicks
  don't have a sense of humor?
Big city: stick it
  to your self-importance!

BUFFALO SURPRISE

On a lonely country road,
gravel,
winding through hills,
along the creeks;
two friends,
a drive of relaxation:

Where does this road go?
What will we see?

Around a curve
suddenly
in the trees—
a herd of buffalo
standing
but too still to be true:
silhouettes with details
accurately painted,
quickly passed—

wishing they were real.

ABSENCE BY INFERENCE

Row of cedar trees
native to the plains
and nearly indestructible,
with a shed behind,
old, ruined,
indicate the absence
of a home
once in the space
the trees protected.
What happened
to this farm?
The missing family?
Tragedy afflicted
on their lives?
And, the children?
What did they feel,
uprooted, scattered,
with the wind?

GARDEN EFFORT

Trees stand tall
in mowed grass
where brush is held at bay.
Space is freedom
to run and play
and avoid the rocks.
Create a garden on a hill,
crazy, madness,
but intense devotion.
Wind blows the trees
and leaves dance,
moonlight streams in silence.
Transformation is the goal,
effort is perfection.
A garden is resulting:
paths, flowers, lawns—
on different elevations,
high and low—
complete.

ON THE HILLSIDE

Buffalo herd on the hillside
  resting
in afternoon heat,
  breathing boulders
scattered in the grass
  and prairie flowers;
more than a hundred—
  awesome sight
and reminder
  of time when
great multitudes
  of the giant beasts
owned the prairie
  past horizon—
source of meat, bone tools,
  tipi skins and more
For Kanza, Lakota
  and others on the plains.

ROAD THROUGH THE TREES

Going somewhere
unknown to me,
road through the trees
narrow, gravel, empty,
as it winds
beside the highway
then disappears—
alluring.
I know where I'm going
on the highway,
routine, well traveled
and predictable,
but that road
through the trees:
where does it go?
I want to go…
Maybe someday
I, too...

STONE SHELL

Rock house stands
alone
in what once was
a front yard,
now pasture
from prairie.
No roof—
long gone,
doors too, and windows.
Did the family take them,
or scavengers, or time?
Red cedars crowd
from the gully in back
marching to invade:
no one keeps their place.
The house had charm,
the lines say that.
Stunted trees say:
poor soil, no crops,
and the family,
future in debt,
moved on
with pain and hope
that next time
will be better.
Next time,
maybe,
it will rain.

THE FULLNESS OF SUMMER

Sunflower glories
along the road
and goldenrod bright
amid dark grass
and other plants
of summer's growth.
Trees dark green
with deep shadows
and bumper crops
approaching harvest.
It was a good year.
There was rain
to fill ponds
and creeks—
refreshing
after years
of drought.
We will survive.

TREE DANCE

Tree glistening
in wet
soft breeze
glittering leaves
dancing
alive
joyful
rejoicing in rain
and summer's day.

ROLLING SEAS

I live not near the ocean
    nor sleep beside its roar.

I live near a different sea
    waves whisper under wind.
Green is when we hear it wash,
    then final golden rustle.

How alike the two seas are
    under blazing sun,
clouds cause each
    to grow in different ways
with life most hidden
    under surface seen.

My sea cycles
    every growing season:
sea of green turns gold,
    waving all the while;
rolling seas of wheat
    make up my prairie ocean.

DAWN LIGHT

Gently waking the world;
   dawn light.
Time for early chores—
   animals stir.

Heart filled with joy
   and gratitude
     for creation
     and Creator,

Farm boy pausing at the gate,
   chants with rising sun:
   Allah'u'Abha,
   Allah'u'Abha,
   Allah'u'Abha.

Another day's begun.

   God is All Glorious,
   He is All Glorious,
    Verily:
   The All Glorious.

TRAVELING

Going to the woods
  with a book,
 sitting on a hill
  with trees for company:
 there is no greater bliss.

The wind moves gently
  across the page,
 birds proclaim their joy
  and shade dabbles
 space around my feet.

I am alone in time
  and eternity,
 with a book I step
  out of my life and place,
 into somewhere else.

Experience expands
  limitations vanish
 imagination soars:
  who knows what I….

CAUGHT IN THE AIR

Suspended,
   with no string,
struggling,
   fluttering,
trying with all its might
   to fly.
All the energy the bird
   expends
is only enough
   to keep it
hanging
   in the same place.
It struggles
   then turns
and dives away
   to freedom,
no longer prisoner
   of the wind.

FLINT HILLS FARM

Ghosts of daughters
and sons,
bringing pails from the barn
with stalls and loft,
to the milk house
cool, of dressed stone.
And, near the back door, eggs,
from the chicken house.
The farm was laid out well—
parlor windows
provided views of all.
But calamity occurred
and the farm was left alone,
weeds and grass grew rank
and cedars over grown.
Deer return once more
to graze and sleep
and—the wind…

SPIRIT OF THE WELL

I know a well
    that lives in the woods,
an old and ancient well
    with moss covered rocks.
The water is not far
    with its power
and says,
    "More, there is more."
I'm held as I wonder
    what is there deep
that pulls me in,
    to rocks with cracks?
What is this primal awe,
    this reverence
for the spirit of the well,
    the water and the moss,
the unknown deep
    that pulls me in?

HAUNTING SUMMONS

That Special Night
I remember
something called me
some power older,
far more ancient,
than civilization,
called me out:
out of my bed,
out of the house,
out to the hill,
away from trees
to full glory
of the amber orb
and its golden light
over waves
of tall grass blowing—
I stood enchanted.
This was a scene
mysterious
hidden from day
the true, full light
of the golden moon
in power and glory.
I am there still,
transfixed,
in awe.
I couldn't resist.

COTTONWOOD

Tree of the plains:
   tall, enormous,
where there is water—
   enough.
Glittering leaves
   tickle the eye
flickering light
   and rustling breeze.
Deeply variegated bark
   speaks its age
and with shade
   most welcome—
on hot, wide
   tree-starved plains.
Horse pulling wagon,
   and family,
aim for the tree:
   cool shade—and rest!

MOVING WATER

There is something about water,
   moving water,
even if the water
     is not all moving,
just ripples across the top—
   it is the motion;
this water answers
     something deep
within ourselves
      we don't even know
yet come back
   again and again and again.
Does the water in us
    (98%)
recognize
   the vast and greater water
that we see
     and know that it is life?

BUFFALO SPIRIT

Giant beasts of the plains
    across the hillside
calmly eating their way
       in one direction.

Calves are mixed in the herd
    with their mothers
who all have horns
       and humps of their age.

Once great multitudes roamed
    these endless seas
of grass and sky,
       great thundering herds.

Now herds are fenced
    and restricted
to places here and there,
       they cannot roam at will.

Still, they remain
    awesome beasts:
awesome and amazing,
       huge and fearsome...

Once indispensable
    to prairie life,
now curiosities,
       a reminder of the past.

They allow our imagination
    to join them in another time,
to become with them
       free spirits and roam   >>>

Over hills and valleys
    of spiritual adventure,
to thunder unrestrained
        through prairies of possibilities.

Buffalo are now a symbol
    of our souls,
to be and grow
        as God intended.

COUNTRY BURIED

Little cemetery
  off the road
through a pasture
  with a gate:
aged stones,
  tilted and worn.
Who were the people?
  Where did they live?
What did they do?
  How did they die?
Graves forgotten
  with passing of time,
their lives and loves
  are lost.
Ripples of their deeds,
  and stones,
only remain
  as evidence.

NIGHT SECRETS

Lying under a starry sky
meteor zooms
streaking silent light—
vanishes.

Wind whispers secrets
rustling grasses, leaves,
faintly to be seen
in bright starlight:
shapes and trees with branches.

Slowly, so slowly,
yellow moon rises
over the distant line
gradually showing itself—
full.

Coyotes yip and howl
here and there.

Prairie night—
has begun.

RURAL CONVERSATION

Car went by t'day.
Really?
Yep.
Who's it?
Don't know.
Don't know?
Nope. Never seen it 'fore.
How odd.
Yep.
Could'a been lost?
Must have.
Think they be back?
Can't 'magine.
Might get lost again…
Not likely.
Big day, wan't it?
I'll say.

Wonder who it could'a been...

TRANSITION

Shadows fall
  across the land
cast by trees
  and barns and houses
as the setting sun
  lowers its horizons
until
  a streak of light
here and there
  is all that one can see
then shadows
  hide the world—
now the moon
  smiles its silver light
full
  in radiant glory
and the world
  is newly seen.

PASTURE GATE

At a junction of three fences
there was a curious
gate configuration
to allow cattle
to be moved
from any one pasture
to any other
in the same space,
but it was hell to drive
a tractor through,
and with baler and hay wagon—
nearly impossible,
yet my father
would inch them all along.
I should have said,
"Let's do it, Dad,
and make one gate."

He died before I could.

SCHOOLHOUSE PICNIC

We had a picnic,
  my children and I,
under bare branches
  in an old schoolyard,
reclaimed by prairie,
  of a forgotten school.
After eating we explored
  the abandon school,
cracked cement stoop,
  no door, but a floor,
walls ripped out
  and birds in rafters.
Outside, bones and fur
  and one outhouse.
Our trip was long,
  the stop was good:
a special event
  we will long remember.

SKY VAST

On the rolling prairie
  a walking speck
observes the sky:
  its vast embrace
surrounding
  all the world
and his own
  insignificance,
an even line encircles
  the world,
hills and valleys below
  where trees and rivers run,
the sky becomes
  a teacher of perspective:
nothing else
  is so huge
and one learns instant
  humility.

POND EXPERIMENT

One stick remained
 of dynamite
from blasting holes
 in rock.
"Come on kids," he cried
 let's see what happens."
Dad lit the fuse and threw
 into the pond.
Awesome muffled, "BOOM!"
 and the pond rose
like a bowl,
 bottom up, with fish.
As the surface leveled
 the fish remained
stunned and motionless:
 that was a surprise!
As they woke
 the pond returned to normal.

WIND BLOWN

Abandon farmhouse,
tilting barn,
dead trees
and flowers gone wild:
all tell-tale signs
of family life
and hopes and dreams
that lived and died.
The well remains
with cemented top
that never again
will give a drop,
and lonesome windmill,
broken parts banging,
is no longer
the source of life.
The farm has died
but wind blows on.

ANCIENT WATER

Ancient water
collected over eons
deep, deep down
below the soil
used now for decades
to irrigate
water-needy crops:
wheat, milo, and more.
Might there be someday
another crop more suited
to this land?
Isn't this just
one more feature
of "use-it-up-
there-is-no-future"
irresponsible
mentality?

RAIN DANCE

Dark, low clouds
  turn summer
into a winter's day,
  cooling hot air.
Deep thunder rumble
  is no surprise.
Suddenly—rain
  pounding like shot
on porch roof tin:
  music after drought.
Children dance in rain
  delight in cold and wet,
adults stand
  soaking in relief
life-saving rain
  came just in time
to save the crops
  and life.

TESTING THE TREE

Sixteen year old
farm boy
wanted to see
if tractor and he
were stronger
than a tree.
It was a small tree
only twenty feet
tall
and half a foot
around.
Up and up and up
he drove.
When front axel
began to jump
off the trunk,
the boy backed down
deciding
the tree was stronger.

Decades later,
a friend remarked:
"God let you live
in hope
that one day
you wouldn't be
so STUPID!"

Maybe, she was right.

FENCE BUILDING

The fence did not divide,
    but united,
    it was a livestock border only:
    to keep them from the crop.
For the brothers, owners,
    who did not always agree,
    it became a joint endeavor—
Each knew what to do:
    digging holes,
    pounding posts,
    stringing wire,
    and fastened at certain heights.
The fence was old,
    and with their father gone,
    badly in need of repair.
After brush was cleared
    it was easier to build a new fence
    and so, together, they worked united.

CHALLENGE OF THE BRIDGE

Driving down the hill
on a rutty gravel road
to antiquated bridge,
one lane,
angled to the road,
gaining too much speed—
to fast to turn
onto the bridge—
crash and drowning loomed.
One last hope:
hit a rut just right
to throw the car
onto the bridge.

WHOMP! CHUNK! THUMP!!

Miraculous success:
car coasted across,
teenage boy would live
to be useful.

THE SKY

If one cannot see the sky
  straight ahead
for one hundred-eighty degrees
  all around
unobstructed and open
  how will you know it's there?

The sky is not a patch of grey
  unseen overhead.
The sky is a presence
  that embraces the earth
and all of creation
  circling round.

This is no puny sky,
  of smoke, soot, or foul smells.
This is the breath of God,
  patent from our Creator.
What other sky
  is real?

TIME HAS TOLD

Grass is high
where once was the yard
and path to the creek
is gone.
Lonely the tree
hangs over the shed
falls on itself
untended.
The barn,
that citadel,
signature,
keeping cattle and feed
for the future
and dreams,
collapsed at last
with a thudding roar.
This vital farm
is now no more.

PRAIRIE BREATH

Trees:
branches are still
lifeless leaves.
It is so HOT!
The air
seems sucked away;
there is no breath.
Birds are silent,
hidden:
too hot to fly,
only insects
make motion.
A sound:
faint, distant,
comes closer.
Something moves!
A breeze arrives—
refreshing relief!

GOLDEN

Golden fields of autumn,
golden hills—
summer has passed
harvest has begun.
The year has turned
and will again,
steady order
of the seasons.
As our lives
have seasons too
to prepare
for the glorious harvest
when seasons end
and we go home.
Learning, learning
is our task
and our harvest
will be glory.

EVENING MEDITATION

Red sun slowly sets
  behind freshly naked trees
covering the hillside
  across the valley field,
clouds approach
  and pass.
With rising moon,
  little ones waken
and tumble in play—
  then they see the moon.
Their attention arrested
  they call and yip,
soon the coyote chorus
  is sounding on all sides.
By the fire one can think:
  this is the same as long ago.
If humans disappeared
  would coyotes know?

SILO SENTINEL

Standing tall, proud...
and alone
silo remains witness
of life past
when a farm was here:
house, barn and out-buildings,
varied forms and uses.
Farm was a factory
producing food,
but now gone, erased.
The tide of farm life passed.
Mechanization,
economy of scale
and computer precision
drove the family away.
Value,
gained or lost?
Only time will tell.

AUTUMN MESSENGERS

Smudge on the horizon
    becomes little wavering lines,
these, in turn, become
    separate flying dots,
eventually the dots
    become geese honking
warning of winter suffering:
    "Make way, make way,
freezing time is coming.
    Flee to warmth and life,"
signals turning year,
    harvest must be gathered,
a year of growth has ended,
    prepare for winter's blast.
The geese have warned us,
    we have not much time
for soon
    we must be snug inside.

TRACES THAT REMAIN

Traces on a stone
   are all that remain
of a life,
   of hopes and joys,
   dreams and defeats;
maybe dates:
   years, maybe more,
and sometimes
   an inscription
   or words.
Men, women,
   children of all ages,
died
   of unknown causes.
Families move,
   leave the land
      and behind,
   leave graves.

NIGHT COMING

Gothic arching branches frame
   autumn evening sky;
     tinge of orange,
     power purples
     shades of red,
     melting white
       into light blue.

As twilight deepens.
   stars appear
   and dot the sky
     which turns to midnight black.

Earth is changed—
   disappeared,
   reformed,
   counterpoint—
     to the world of day.

Night...
     has come.

DECISION TO HONOR

The way through the trees,
    two tracks with grass,
curves gently up
    with no hint
of destination
    or end.
Do I follow?
    What lies beyond?
Old farm buildings?
    Or, an empty field?
Do I have time now
    for adventure?
Or, keep the promise
    already made?
My word is my honor:
    I can't today,
But some day—
    I will explore...

OCTOBER FOREVER!

Golden days of golden light,
   golden leaves fall gently
      from the trees
Nights are cool and insects,
   frozen at first frost—
      are gone!
Golden days,
   will turn the seasons
      and a year.
Glorious days
   not long enough
      to enjoy and savor.
If half a year could be October
   I would not mind
      the rest.
Golden light is treasured—
   all too soon:
      will be winter dark.

NO MOUNTAIN LIONS

There are, "No
   mountain lions in Kansas."
At least that
   is official word.

But:
   when you hear two call
     and answer up the creek,
   smell
     their distinctive scent,
   see paw prints
     in pond-shore mud,
   watch one lope
     along the crest of a hill,
   see a pair of cubs
     under a pasture tree...

Who is to question
   the official word:
     they are not here?

AUTUMN WIND SPEAKS

Wind in trees
  in autumn,
going branch to branch,
  is different
from wind in trees
  with leaves;
wind in bare branches:
  a deeper, solid,
more substantial sound
  than whispering in leaves.
It is more definite,
  more determined;
and speaks
  to a deeper level
our self,
  our soul.
I sit in autumn
  and wait for wind.

LONELY LAND

Six outbuildings
one, a small barn,
no house
and just one tree;
obviously once
there was a house
and, likely, more trees—
and flowers.
A family farm
but family is gone
and farming too,
just grassland now.
Soil too poor,
or insufficient rain,
to sustain a farming life,
or improvident decisions,
or a banker's greed,
ended hope.

SEEDS

Bare trees,
branches gray and stark,
grasses dead and standing
all around.
Skies are gray and close.
All is desolate
but
unseen, are secrets,
secrets even we are unaware:
potentials and abilities
we've not even dreamed—
we have inside.
It is challenge, difficulties, and tests
that prompts potential
to actuality.
We can be
most fully us
only
after arising to conditions
unexpected and extreme.
We can praise
the Creator of All
for blessings and ability
to grow.

AUTUMN AFTERNOON

Arches overhead—
    whisper sets in motion,
    a low, cool sun
    shortens afternoons.
Grass is green and gold and brown,
    crickets are all dead;
    the silence rings.
    A lone bird cries:
"It is over, all gone, ended."
    Life is over for a turn,
    turn the world slowly—
    the sun has set.
Dark clouds rolling over,
    wind is cold.
    Time to go in
    for the winter wait.

REMAINING WITNESS

Rock shell of a house—
stepping through the doorway
onto dirt
at one time beneath the floor,
only bits of joists remain,
wood rotted now.
No roof or window frames,
rock is all that's left.
A cottage that had charm,
I see in my mind,
now empty, alone,
yard overgrown,
out-buildings gone
and neighbors too!
Once was a home with love
now coyotes prowl
and deer feed
on abundant grass

Duane L. Herrmann

CLEARING CEDARS

Dry winter day
  is best for this job,
knee pads helpful,
  gloves essential,
and long sleeves—
  a winter guarantee.
Cutting is easiest
  when trees are small;
just inches tall
  is best of all.
Cut even
  with the dirt
stubs will still
  stab tires.
Without this effort
  a cedar forest
will consume
  farmland.

WINTER WET

Trees dripping,
   dark grey branches
against light grey
   clouded sky,
above dead grass
   tawny and beige
stretching miles and miles
   of rolling prairie,
farmsteads nestled
   in creek valleys.
A mild winter
   brings no ice
and only occasional
   snow.
Buffalo don't mind
   nor deer, nor geese.
Only farmers
   worry over moisture.

MY FATHER'S EYES

There is a highway
my father drove
when I was small,
our special time
together:
just me and Daddy—
the only thing
we did together.
I now drive that way
to see
what his eyes saw
and see changes:
it joins our lives.
He's been gone
decades now.
What would he think
of changes
we have seen?

BLUEBIRD WINTER

They went south for winter
and we are far enough.

They settled in the trees
near my office window.

Five or six of them,
entertained all winter.

They flew and flitted
from tree to branch;

Splashes of color
against the winter drab.

I had a bluebird once,
standing on my desk.

I gazed, fascinated,
and painted it exact.

Now, out my window,
I watch real ones—entranced.

Magic
Come to life!

SNOW FALLING

Each perfect star—
six points
miniature perfection
uncreateable by hands
multitudinous abundance
and every one unique,
absorbs all sound
as they float down
blanketing sounds
and ground;
presence here today
melted tomorrow.
To stand in snow fall
is to stand in silence,
hushed the world
and be in awe
of this:
winter's miracle.

SNOW MAKES CLEAR

Even a slight dusting,
  less than half an inch,
of snow reveals
  features of the landscape
that otherwise
  are hidden:
a path in the grass,
  an old road here,
a rail grade there,
  a house foundation.
Amazing
  what the contrast,
the purity of snow,
  can expose.
What contrasts,
  or innocence,
can reveal
  other secrets in life?

WINTER RODENT DREAMS

Curled up safe
in prairie home
I sleep the winter away
I dream of summer runs
through tunnels grass,
some stored here
for this long sleep.
It's not safe
to be topside
while blizzards rage,
there is no cover
for protection
and my kits
need be safe beside.
Come summer sun
we will run,
enjoy new grass
and live above.

FIRE IN THE SNOW

Gently falling snow
    melting in the heat,
yellow leaping flames
    pushing back the cold:
an amazing combination
    of opposites.
The gentle hiss of drops
    falling on the fire
compliments the creek
    gurgling away.
Silent countryside is broken
    by one lonely crow
and a tiny flock of geese
    passing overhead;
two brothers tending wood
    to feed the fire,
cutting cedars
    to keep the pasture clean.

SNOW REVEALS

Highlighted by the snow
the old rail bed
level, straight and true,
across the countryside,
shows the way
once traveled,
hidden otherwise
by trees and green,
the winter shows
the once-used trail
a glimpse
of civilization past.
Goodness also sometimes
is hidden just the same
and is revealed
when circumstances change.
Opportunities
can surprise us.

IN THE SNOW

Spot of red in the snow—
    tiny, isolated:
        easy to be missed.
An eternal event,
    of minor proportions,
        has occurred here.
Tracks across the snow—
    little ones end,
        larger ones continue.

FIRE IN SNOWLIGHT

Magical air
filled with snow
falling, blowing.
Light fragmented, refracted, diffuse
surrounding and embracing
the world.
Trees tall and stark
against gray sky.
Numinous light
reveals
bright, untrod path
of glistening snow.
Fire dances,
as fire does,
flames leap, flicker
and warm.
Enchanting night
not soon repeated.

WARNING

Ruined shed,
  still and low
  falling pieces down.

Farm life ended,
  dreams are dead and gone.
  A single tree remains.

Desolation speaks
  of hard times,
  and imbalance...

"Regard must be paid
  to agriculture.
  It procedeth others..."

Wisdom words
  Unheeded:
  society dies.

Wind bends dead grass and weeds,
  air is cold and dry,
  a year and life are gone.

THE FLOWER DREAMS

Blossom wanted to open
greet the sun
feel rain
dance with wind,
but it deplored
that it could not.
Try as it might
restrictions all around
kept it closed.
Eventually the flower
resigned itself to wait:
it could only dream
of sun
and rain
and wind.
It waited,
unaware the plant
was still a seed.

TOO COLD

Who can write a poem
about a cold,
icy gray
windy day?
Maybe,
if snug and warm inside,
one can write about that
with a good book;
but, being out
with the stinging wind
and ice,
there is little joy
and no delight
on the wild
empty plains
when I'd rather be
warm and safe
at home!

WAITING FOR SPRING

Little pond
   in the meadow
covered half with ice
   is waiting
for the willow to bloom
   on its bank,
and the cattails
   to burst their seeds,
and frogs to crawl
   from their safe place
and sing the joy
   of Spring!
That day will come
   when hearts will melt
and faith will shine
   from every face
and Spring will glow
   in every heart.

HAUNTING HOPE OF SPRING

Winter is over, or
  at least one can think so,
yet
  the garden is still dead.
The haunting hope of Spring
  floats in the air
over the lingering dead
  leaves and stalks,
No new green in sight—
  just expectation.
It is that awkward time
  when winter can return
and Spring is not yet
  confident to appear.
New life is stirring
  in the world
and in the soil,
  waiting to be born.

NOTES

Family Plowing: The word "machineries" is a term used by the author's grandfather to refer to all farm equipment too large to carry by hand—any kind of machinery. If it could be carried by hand it was a tool. This poem was selected for inclusion in "Kansas Poets Trail" in downtown Wichita.

Grandfather's Road: This poem is the result of a mistake. The author had found the correct property, but was on the wrong boundary road. He later found the correct road—the line of stones, some bits broken glassware and the front yard fence. On his next trip all that had been cleared away.

Dawn Light: "Allah'u'Abhá," a form of the title: Bahá'u'lláh, meanings given in the poem.

My Father's Eyes: When the author was 16, his father died as the result of a serious medical mistake while successfully recovering from a tractor accident.

Warning: Quoted - Bahá'u'lláh, Tablet of the World, *Tablets of Bahá'u'lláh (Haifa: Bahá'í World Center, 1978), p.90.*

INDEX OF TITLES

Absence by Inference, 33
Ancient Water, 60
Autumn Afternoon, 80
Autumn Messengers, 71
Autumn Wind Speaks, 77
Barn Remains, 30
Bluebird Winter, 85
Buffalo Spirit, 49
Buffalo Surprise, 32
Builders of Barns, 27
Caught in the Air, 43
Challenge of the Bridge, 64
Chicken Creek Road, 4
Clearing Cedars, 82
Cottonwood, 47
Country Buried, 51
Coyote Rules the World, 16
Dawn Light, 41
Decision to Honor, 74
Evening Meditation, 69
Family House, The, 11
Family Plowing, 1
Fence Building, 63
Fire in Snowlight, 92
Fire in the Snow, 89
Flint Hills Farm, 44
Flower Dreams, The, 94
For Deer Waiting, 23
Fullness of Summer, The, 38
Garden Effort, 34
Golden, 68
Grandfather's Barn, 22
Grandfather's Road, 2
Haunting Hope of Spring, 97
Haunting Summons, 46
House on the Edge of a
    Meadow, 8
In the Snow, 91
Kansas Nachtlied, Goethe, 17
Lonely Land, 78
Lost Road, 13
Magic Evening, 12

Making Hay, 21
Moving Water, 48
My Father's Eyes, 84
Next Five Exits, 31
Night Coming, 73
Night Necklaces, 6
Night Secrets, 52
No Mountain Lions, 76
October Forever!, 75
On the Hillside, 35
On the Horizon, 26
Pasture Gate, 55
Pigs in a Blanket, 7
Plowing Lesson, 15
Pond Experiment, 58
Prairie Breath, 67
Prairie Hawk, 19
Rain Dance, 61
Remaining Witness, 81
Road Through the Trees, 36
Rolling Seas, 40
Rural Conversation, 53
Schoolhouse Picnic, 56
Seeds, 79
Silo Sentinel, 70
Sky Vast, 57
Sky, The, 65
Sleeping to the Sound of
    Rain, 29
Snow Falling, 86
Snow Makes Clear, 87
Snow Reveals, 90
Song of the Prairie Night, 24
Spirit of the Well, 45
Spring Lake, 3
Spring Towers, 5
Stone Shell, 37
Summer Wetting, 18
Testing the Tree, 62
Time Has Told, 66
Tiny Pond, 14
Too Cold, 95

Traces that Remain, 72
Transition, 54
Traveling, 42
Tree Dance, 39
Unnatural Mark, 28
Wagon Tale, 25
Waiting for Spring, 96
Warning, 93
Wind Blown, 59
Wind's Own, The, 9
Winter Rodent Dreams, 88
Winter Wet, 83
Witness, 20

INDEX OF FIRST LINES

Abandon building, 20
Abandon farmhouse, 59
After the war of 1812, 13
Ancient water, 60
Arches overhead, 80
As he trots across the field, 16
At a junction of three fences, 55
Bare trees, 79
Blossom wanted to open, 94
Buffalo herd on the hillside, 35
Car went by t'day, 53
Curled up safe, 88
Dark, low clouds, 61
Driving down the hill, 64
Driving down the rocky road, 25
Dry winter day, 82
Each perfect star, 86
Even a light dusting, 87
fence did not divide, The, 63
Gently falling snow, 89
Gently waking the world, 41
Ghosts of daughters, 44
Giant beasts of the plains, 49
Glittering strings, 6
Going to the woods, 42
Going somewhere, 36
Golden days of golden light, 75
Golden fields of autumn, 68
Gothic arching branches frame, 73
Grandmother engineered the
    evening, 12
Grass is high, 66
Heat had been forever, 18
Highlighted by the snow, 90
Howling, calling, 24
I live not near the ocean, 40
I know a well, 45
I plow the paper with a pen, 1
I sought refuge, 11
I was fourteen, 15
If one cannot see the sky, 65
In twilight time, 23

Invisible to the traveler now, 2
Little cemetery, 51
Little pond, 96
Lying under a starry sky, 52
Magical air, 92
Mornings when the dew had
    dried, 21
My grandfather's barn, 22
No one would know, 14
No up-scale suburb, this!, 4
Not a blanket, actually, 7
On a lonely country road, 32
On the rolling prairie, 57
On the small state highway, 31
On the vast dry plains, 29
One stick remained, 58
Over the fields and prairie, 19
Red sun slowly sets, 69
Rock house stands, 37
Rock shell of a house, 81
Row of cedar trees, 93
Ruined shed, 93
Shadows fall, 54
Sitting on the rocks, 3
Six outbuildings, 78
Sixteen year old, 62
Smudge on the horizon, 71
Spot of red in the snow, 91
Standing tall, proud, 70
Straight line, 28
Sunflower glories, 38
Suspended, 43
That Special Night, 46
There are, "No, 76
There is a highway, 84
There is a house, 8
There is a stillness, 17
There is something about
    water, 48
They knew, 27
They went south for winter, 85
Towers of the Spring, 5

Trace on a stone, 72
Tree glistening, 39
Tree of the plains, 47
Tree on the rise of the prairie, 26
Trees dripping, 83
Trees have grown around it
     now, 30
Trees stand tall, 34
Trees, 67
way through the trees, The, 74
We had a picnic, 56
Who can write a poem, 95
Wind in trees, 77
Wind, 9
Winter is over, or, 97

PUBLICATION CREDITS

Ampersand Lit.: Song of the Prairie Night.

Blue Pen: Unnatural Mark.

In Praise of Prairies: The Flower Dreams, The Fullness of Summer, Tree Dance, Cottonwood, Stone Shell.

Little Balkans Review: Flint Hills Farm.

Manifest West: Next Five Exits.

Midwest Quarterly: On the Hillside.

Orison: No Mountain Lions.

Prairies of Possibilities: Chicken Creek Road, Family Plowing, Fire in the Snow, Making Hay, On the Horizon, Prairie Hawk, Rolling Seas, Summer Wetting, Wagon Tale, Waiting for Spring.

Peacock Journal: Challenge of the Bridge, Testing the Tree, Plowing Lesson.

Perspectives Magazine: Winter Rodent Dreams.

Planet Kansas: Ancient Water, Found, Hidden in Plain Sight, Lost Road, Rejoicing.

Rose Red Review: Tiny Pond.

theliteraryyard.com*:* Snow Falling

Tiny Seed: Tree Dance

Topeka Genealogical Society Quarterly: Barn Remains, Country Buried, Decision to Honor, Road Through the Trees, Silo Sentinel, Stone Shell, Traces That Remain.

Voices from a Borrowed Garden: Grandfather's Road.

Wagon Magazine: Buffalo Surprise, Night Necklaces, Wind Blown.

Whispers Shouting Glory: Autumn Afternoon, Coyote Rules the World, Dawn Light, For Deer Waiting, House on the Edge of a Meadow, In the Snow, Night Coming, Spring Lake, Spring Towers, The Wind's Own.

Write On!: Too Cold.

Zingara: Absence by Inference.

ABOUT THE AUTHOR

Duane L Herrmann was born in Topeka, Kansas, in 1951 and grew up on a nearby farm. Beginning at age two and a half he was expected to share in the care of his younger siblings and chores. This increasingly progressed to age thirteen when he managed the house half the summer while his mother was away. When she returned he was put on a tractor to begin farming. He farmed until his father was killed the year before he left home for college. Away from home he discovered and embraced the Bahá'í Faith. And, he began to write in earnest; at home that had been forbidden.

His first poems were published in 1969 when a senior in high school. Also that year his drama teacher wanted to produce the play he wrote for a class project. In college his first news articles and more poems were published. In 1974 he married, which produced four children but little writing.

In 1986, after he had built the house his family lived in, he achieved his first commercial sale. In 1989 his first book, as well as his first chapbooks of poetry, were published and he received the Robert Hayden Poetry Fellowship. The marriage ended, but he continued to be very active in his children's lives and wrote more.

His poetry, histories, memoirs, fiction, and children's stories have appeared in a dozen countries in four languages and can be found in libraries on three continents. He is increasingly cited and quoted in print and social media. He has received prizes or recognition from the Kansas State Poetry Society, Kansas Authors Club, Writers Matrix, Ferguson Kansas History Book Award, Kansas Poets Trail, Kansas State Historical Society, and Map of Kansas Literature. Not bad for a dyslexic with ADD, cyclothymia, and PTSD!

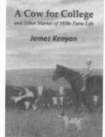

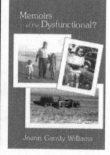

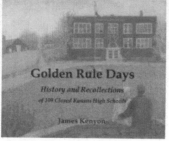

www.birdypoetryprize.com

Meadowlark Books created The Birdy Poetry Prize to celebrate the voices of this era. Cash prize, publication, and 50 copies awarded annually.

Entries Accepted: May 1 to December 1.

Final Deadline for Entries: December 1, midnight.

Entry Fee: $25

All entries will be considered for standard Meadowlark Books publishing contract offers, as well.

Full-length poetry manuscripts (55 page minimum) will be considered. Poems may be previously published in journals and/or anthologies, but not in full-length, single-author volumes. All poets are eligible to enter, regardless of publishing history.

See the website, meadowlark-books.com, for complete submission guidelines.

Read

A Meadowlark Book

Nothing feels better than home

meadowlark-books.com

While we at Meadowlark Books love to travel, we also cherish our home time. We are nourished by our open prairies, our enormous skies, community, family, and friends. We are rooted in this land, and that is why Meadowlark Books publishes regional authors.

When you open one of our fiction books, you'll read delicious stories that are set in the Heartland. Settle in with a volume of poetry, and you'll remember just how much you love this place too—the landscape, its skies, the people.

Meadowlark Books publishes memoir, poetry, short stories, and novels. Read stories that began in the Heartland, that were written here. Add to your Meadowlark Book collection today.

Specializing in Books by Authors from the Heartland Since 2014

Made in the USA
Middletown, DE
29 October 2021